When I Forget
The Words

Poems by

Linda Lobmeyer

darkly bright press

When I Forget The Words
Poems by Linda Lobmeyer

Catalog Number 021

ISBN: 979-8-9899449-2-7

Library of Congress Control Number: 2024942048

darkly bright
press & design

www.darklybrightpress.com

Table of Contents

For My Parents

Part One

Sight Reading

Every Days

These are days we will never
measure nor remark upon
winters without blizzard
cold without ice.

Days that whittle. We do
not recognize the knife
carving away slim slivers
of ordinary time.

Shavings fall like days from
a calendar when what
we held tightly
now softly we behold.

Unable to pinpoint
the hour, day, month when what
was shapeless and without form
became important and true.

If we are fortunate
we will say, *it was a warm
day, but a cool morning.*
It must have been winter.

We will consider the new thing
made by the quiet hand
of passing days, and hold
what we cannot now live without.

The Violent

There will come a day when
Flannery O'Connor
will begin to make sense.

Instead of feeling charmed,
appalled. You will
see yourself drowning

someone you love—will know
something you did not know
before. You were always

the goat. Always among
those ordered to depart,
separated.

In spite of the moments
you thought yourself so grand,
your gift the most selfless.

You will see yourself as you are:
a greedy thief, lustful liar,
the story's villain.

Mercy will stop
being your gift, but the
thing you beg for.

Strange Parts

Read the strange parts again,
the parts you believed
you believe until you
can't make out their meaning

When He asks
Will you leave too?
Answer him—*Where?*
Where could I go?

On that day, when
what is true is revealed
you will be asked (out loud)
for your assent (out loud)

When you answer
your weak knees
will become firm
in your feeble heart.

Maybe on some beach
over a fire you'll eat
fish at sunrise, and we'll
talk about the strange parts

now in my throat
now on my knees
here are the words
Where could I go?

What You Want

What you want
    isn't what you're given

the wild thunderstorm,
    your prayer for rain

hoping you wouldn't lose
    that cedar to drought

you never wanted
    a clash of thunder waking you

two in the morning
    eyes open, thinking about tomorrow

no gentle rain
    falling as you dream

if you weren't awake
    during the dark sleeping time

you would never
    have imagined the path

to the sleeping dream
    you had forgotten

This Year's Tulips

Tucked safely in the earth
a scratch of hope in drought
memory clinging to
moisture and warm sunbeams

emerging from the soil
stubby with want and need
they push forth their red blooms
as bright ere any were

they did their year's work with
stocky resolution
exposed to April's bite
shocking the resolute

red tulips with iced wind
and unexpected snow
coating their blooms in white
suffering spring's wild joys.

Some Know

Some know the worst thing
some have their guesses
some have never considered
not knowing is a blessing.

Them that know the worst things
wait for something worse
they fret, but are surprised by
the catastrophic slings.

Those happy unknowing
neither worry nor whine
their hearth and home restful
their dog sleeping like mine.

Dust Storm

Wednesday's dust storm
distorts the sky
blue to orange (not sunset)

the color of an empty field
boots covered in quarter section
after all the crops die

a hand over brow shades
creased eyes fixing a gaze
on the next grain elevator

twenty miles away
under this corner of Kansas
a distance unobstructed

a hopeful space
a resigned monotony
no matter how dull

our endless blue sky
our vision so clear
we reckon there's no conflict

headlights on at noon
we can't expect
to see every day

visibility swallows the earth
covering highway eighty-three
like a familiar bowl

we'll forget Wednesday when
vision returns and no storm
blinds our sight

eternity will follow us,
forever, like the grain elevator
in the distance.

Brief Showers Followed by Sun

Leaving work for the day it seems
it rained for a moment this afternoon.

I've wasted another day or feel I did
not knowing what a good day should be.

I am a brief rain, hoping to reveal
all that churns in my clouds

Did the rain wonder who she should be?
Did her questions cause her to sputter

so abruptly that she gathered herself
hoping that no one would notice her?

If the rain knew what a good day
should be, could she drench the earth

with all she believes possible
unveiling the bloom of spring?

October Rains

Rain falls softly in perfection
a cool reprieve after a hot
summer.

My father fell last night
in this, his ninety-first October.
I know

pleasant days are fleeting
but promise to return. Waking
this morning

to the sound of falling rain, I linger
under the covers, trying to
forget

his dark fear on the floor unable
to help him back into his bed.
When I

rise, I peek into his bedroom.
He sleeps like a little boy,
peaceful

no memory of forgetting
how to stand or who I am.
I stand

in the doorway staring through his
window. I watch the falling rain,
leaves drift

from the trees like days. Soon they will
be bare, their life hidden by winter.
We wait

for life's promise to return.

The Persistence of Ivy

The spry leaf on the severed stem clings
to the sharp blade of the garden shears
unaware of its separation, a casualty
of the war with the ivy on the north side
of the house.

Growing in spite of the inhospitable
shadow. The vine roots
itself around my house
breaking through
the concrete of the back step. It climbed
through the basement window
oblivious to the implicit repulsion,
it breaks through
with a steady, slow push
wandering into the sweet peas
hiding among the welcome leaves.

Even these I considered killing
my first year at the house
questioning the leaves, but
concluding by on-line sleuthing
these were perennial sweet peas.
Now I lift their leafy arms onto the garden
fence helping the coils attach twining,
climbing. The flowers freckle the house
with pink and white.

The persistent ivy spreading
itself near the ground
battling for its right to stay
recalling a gentle planting
in shallow shadow of turned soil
with no promise of growth. Fighting
to become this bushy, green vine.

I reach into the soft, leafy sweet peas
to find a root of ivy. I yank a rough brown stem
to find its origin and surround it with
 the bladed "V", shearing the ivy to the earth.
There you go, Sweet Pea.
All yours.

Debris

for Dolores

Everyone says they don't remember
a summer so hot, even Dolores
in her eighties. She's lived here since
nineteen-forty something.

This evening I find her
carrying yard debris
to the dumpster: flowers
that once bloomed, stalks that grew
toward the sun, now refuse

succumbing
to long days and
wasting heat.

She lost her husband this winter
when days are never long enough.
Alone now, she tells me again
of the day he died
the way she told me
the day he died.

I've heard it so often
I imagine his body
on the linoleum,
the confusion of flashing lights
from the ambulance and police,
waiting for her children to come home.

She and I again
recall his death, sitting at the kitchen table
taking a break from carrying
debris, during this hot summer
of new memory filled with heat
brittle with solitude.

For Saint Veronica

Unclean, diseased, outside
I have seen your face in my heart
wept exile with your tears

I sought a doctor's cure
in my century without needing
to grasp healing.

We have spoken often without meeting
Sister saint, were you childless too?
Now whole, the years still gone.

You knew the Savior by his work
fallow wonder replaced by miracle
his hem like cooked fish on the beach,

bread and wine on Thursday
all the decay redeemed
the food he ate, the clothes he wore.

Your veil cleaning his face
leaving a stain in blood.
I pause at station six.

What was unholy and unclean
sanctified like the water of
baptism. The flesh which

He spoke into being, then clothed
Himself in so that we, the unclean,
could touch His hem.

Groundhog Day

Despite its nearness
to the Savior's birth
January exiles us
in chilled despair
chaps hands and face

inside we
crack and shatter
gloving our hands
noosing our necks
with scarves, booted

scruffy tracks pursue us
through the dusty snow
we search for a sprig
of green through
bleary eyes

and slip toward February
as the sun's stay
lengthens our days
hope sparks
recalling a bonfire

and the return of
God's glory
first observed by
Simeon, and today
by the lowly groundhog

escaping the shadow
let us men
eat our pancakes
and regard the light
of the world.

Part Two

Practice

What the Neighbors See

God and me, we try real hard
to feel like we're enough
to show the world how God
favors his children, but
something about my neighbor
makes me feel alone.

I try, God and me, and
my neighbor tries, God and he,
to stop eating hatred
biting and devouring, but
it's work to love, so much work.
We can't do it alone.

In my eyes my neighbor sees
his own struggle reflected to him,
something I cannot see
cannot know, a burden as tall
as a mountain near my own sea
he bears alone without me.

My neighbor and me, we
were born together, always
with one another, connected
by a garden, a sin,
a crucifixion. Even so,
we perceive solitude.

In my neighbor's eyes
I see reflected a cataclysm,
a tiny big bang exploding
inside of me, reminding me
of how little I am, how slow
I move, like a rock cliff shifting
into a sandy beach.

I work alone, so diligent,
to be more than my neighbor
so I can know that God has
blessed me. By this work
I best love my neighbor
without inconvenience
on my road to Jericho.

Walls

Here is your wall
you cannot move through it

here are three more
the walls will enclose you

somewhere a dam
breaks, water fills the room

do not panic
the water buoys you

look up, see sky
nothing is above you

as the room fills
the water you thought would

kill you, lifts you
swim yourself to the edge

pull yourself out
and stand atop the wall

above it now
what once was your ending

the wall you wished
to punch your fist into

reveals your life

Silence

Isn't it just like the silence
still and static
acting like it can't hear
all the noises it makes
when I'm trying to think?

Isn't it just like a page
to be content with empty
wordless and white
forcing me to write
witless words to cover it up?

In the café,
I can't hear the words
over all the music.
If I could end
the silence on the page

to let someone else read
to me the words,
his comments filling
the silence,
worthy of my response.

Saint Sebastian in the Kitchen

Dicing the onion and pressing the garlic,
butter bubbles, simmers in the skillet
the smell of warm, home and heartbeats skipping
against my chest like the ticking of time
searching the spice rack for thyme, I'm stirring.

The aroma recalls my own record.
I close my eyes and see Saint Sebastian
pinned with arrows, miraculous alive,
later clubbed to death in the sewers.
I stop and wonder what's at the bottom
of the drain, overcome by a steady stink.

No one cleans up the symbolic spills.
The kids think the canned version is as good
as anything they have ever tasted.
New recipes take the place of the ones
we can't follow. Lucy's eyes circle the plate.

The meal on the table, splitting my apron
with a sharpened knife half for me and half
for the starving cloud of witnesses.
Saint Martin of Tours is praying for us
before the meal half as warm as before.

After we've eaten and without a word,
we sing songs without voice, solitary
in our daily routine, an exchange
of excess goods, many plastic bells ring,
but no one hears the call for the Angelus.

Saint Cecelia's voice rises from her bath,
muted by the machinations of the dishwasher.
Watching my own reflection in the window,
I turn away, over-nourished, not pretty enough
to escape the pride that lands you in hell.

And beneath the altars, they pray for us,
singing with me even when
I forget the words as I'm
strapped to a rack of satiety
and unused beliefs like a jar
of molasses, opaque on the shelf,
neglected,
forgotten,
half-empty.

Pray for us.

Neutral

Our dreams come true
now achieved
feel frumpy and old
*These walls are not
the right color anymore.*

The house and its bells
are gnats infesting our peace.
The backyard oasis
billed as retreat is toil
by the sweat of our brow.

Living to want
we can't stop being evil.
Dissatisfied with what we
thought we needed
having it all, the wants shift.

A common covetousness
in our empty homes.
The fixed dripping faucet
becomes the wrong sink
becomes the quartz countertops
the remodel, the one more room,
the walk-in closet to hold
all of the things.

The moment we walk in
we step into a deeper need
waiting for one of us to stop
to sit still in an open space
quiet in a sunbeam
a bit of nothing until
we breathe a clean breath
content and satisfied.

Fallen

The gravity of today
pulled me
       down
               down
                       down
to the terrestrial origins
of all who walk
trapped by the spinning.

Here among the masses
in whom life was breathed
I exhale nothing special.

We all stare at our feet
accusing our spirts
tied to the ground.

The masses and I
once spoke to the sky—
we heard an answer.

We fell
and realized everything
is silence.

We, who were made
with stars,
formed in goodness
deprived of our garden,
crawl starving
and thirsty.

Examen

I recommend she seek
the serpent's opinion
when Eve asks me
about the best fruit.

I splash around
during the flood, kicking
at the carcasses
and drinking rainwater.
*I hope your boat sinks
and your whole family drowns.*

I saw a bush on fire in the desert,
I put in my earbuds
and laced up my new running shoes.

I'm the first one to tell Moses
the manna tastes
like sand in my mouth.

I bow to idols
I eat dinner with the King.

I clap with delight
when Salome receives
the severed head.

This new dress?
I got it on sale,
only thirty pieces of silver.

The serpent takes
all the credit, but
I helped him plan the whole thing.

Drizzle in the Flint Hills

If scars were drizzle
and memories the freeze
could I scrape out vision
onto my life's windshield?

Could the defrost setting
dislodge the misty pain
sticking as I drive south?

Sleet pelts and frosts tallgrass
white upon red and tan
above the slow greening

grass braves the falling ice
strong, deep roots spread treelike
under the earth, holding

steady against the fickle wind
gripping the soil tight.
Dig deep and grow hidden

in the soil's warmth. Expose
your tender green to May.
Grow tall and marry the sky.

Detonation

In every tick of time
we hear eternity
made of God and us
that never ends

we create
for we were created
we decay as
we hasten from the creator

I watch bombs explode again.

youth run from joy to grief
where is God?
we want to know,
was He not there?

or, if present did not
detonate this will
but held those who would
leave us and find rest.

Our brother, this son of Adam
tried to grip time in his hands
fill eternity with something
bigger than God

unaware

He is smaller than the ticking,
too liquid for human hands
too big to be outdone by death
so timid and deformed.

Better than Nothing

Eating my lunch alone
nothing poetical happens
I blame myself.

Once I stood against the wind
let it howl in my ear
believed it a sign from on high

at least some temptation
from the devil to think
it all revolves around my feelings.

The wind gave me a gift
a confidence that I can
find meaning anywhere

even in a sandwich
but, not today.
I observe no subtle ironies

no play on words
no symbols
no thread of meaning

not even a tomorrow
where we laugh about it
it's just my roast beef sandwich

and it tastes ok
slightly better than nothing.

Cardboard Box

Far away
closer than my breath
near me
still and moving

together tearing and dreaming
until my heartbeat and your hand
are as big Jupiter and nearer
than the weight of glory
you keep shoving me toward
resisting, I beg for the thing
I'm certain I need

Your empty cardboard box
contains more than the gifts
I demand wrapped in gold paper.

Instead

Make something of each one
gather them like rainfall
the we's that don't become
us's and the ones that
stagnate in wasted pools

the disappointing hopes
you attain, the dreams you
neglect. Ignore the fiends
who smell salty despair
drown a little inside

reach for the shore like waves
so far from your center
close your eyes praying
that tomorrow you'll be
closer. Ask stubby eyelashes

to dam the tears. Ink this
body into a poem
and read it to a room
let them wander from you
let them try to swim near.

Suck in breaths together.
Arrive. Stand on the warm
dry shore. Hold someone's hand
look up at the blue sky
which is never wicked.

To Michael Higgins as He Leaves Kansas

I've tried to make this poetic
for you. Life is an empty jar.
You can fill it with what you want.

You might collect buttons or coins.
You might can some spaghetti sauce.
You should use what's put in your jar.

Invite your friends for a meal. Sew
buttons to save your Hawaiian
shirt. Add your pennies, see a movie.

Don't be hopeless when it's empty.
That's how it started. Refill it.
Wash out your jar and make it clean.

Fill it with pretty things, treasures,
shells or jam.   Use the giant pots
in your kitchen.   Walk on the beach.

Fill the jar with what it good. Make
biscuits. Tell someone about the
broken shell you found on the shore.

Show her the prettiest thing you
saved in your jar. Ask if she has
one too.

Part Three

Duets

Will it always repeat

like a ripple
in still water
repeating itself
in smaller and
smaller waves

Do you believe
that if your sight
were infinite
you could
perceive the circle
eternally?

I am liquid
your smile a stone
I begin to ripple
when I see you
staring at me.

The Room Where I Feel Safe

Is there a room
where I am safe?
Alone
no wants or needs
fully alive
fully without
these burdensome brown eyes

able to talk nonsense
laughing at my own jokes
a society in my mind
no hot tears of longing
or angel voices saying no
not resenting
my younger self

that voiceless girl
who bit her tongue
wallpaper silence
always fading
into shadow

skin-pricked by swift thin pins

The Moon is Breathing

*"Observations of the Moon…
confirm the presence of OH/H2O
on the lunar surface…"*

--astronomer Jessica Sunshine

The moon is breathing,
so Sunshine says, beaming
her light toward her planets

and satellites, each one
echoing back her glow
her light stark bright

revealing space
particles
clouds and rings

landing warm and yellow
like this sunbeam
on my small face

the moon takes a full breath
revealing his secret water
on earth I sit in the sunshine

by a green pond barefoot
dipping my toes in the cool moss
the exhalation of the moon

must feel like this breeze, rustling
the cottonwoods. Maybe
the sunshine feeling the Moon's breath

on her face, his presence pulling
at her beam. The moon's dampish air
on her fire, giving her hope

that her light does not shine in vain.
The way I feel chosen
on this hot summer day

in the sunshine with cool water
at my feet and breath
in the trees.

The Difference

for Michael and Lea Ann

Not what this isn't.
Not what this is.
It is the difference.

You once ran through
heavy beach sand
slow and unsteady.

You reach the shore
the heavy sand lapped
by ocean waves

this ground is sturdy
leaving you free
to run, having

swallowed the tides'
kisses, this sand strong
enough to build castles.

She Doesn't Need a Poem
for Lainey

White- gowned bride, heart swollen
beyond hope to belief
passed knowing

no conflict in this girl
too naïve to construe
her promise

promising her whole heart
a whole life as youth hides
her crow's feet

from tears not yet fallen
and sorrows yet to come
no safe dream

in his eyes she sees life
and in her life she sees
heedless joys

she and he will be lone
witnesses to what God
welds and joins

his I do to her yes
her I do an I will
her efforts

are of course, love becomes
their own, she runs to him
without shoes.

Second Date

During intermission
of this play you have seen,
knowing it will bore you
as the man you are with
begins to bore you too

do not order coffee
the wine was made for you
for this moment so that
you will know that the Lord
has not abandoned you.

Crossing the International Dateline

Together
we speak of
futures that
still us with
fear that dreams
will never
become true.

Tomorrow
drives you
away to
an airport
where we drink
coffee, hug, say
I love you.

Tearing I
bite my lip
your flight climbs
skipping to
tomorrow
safe landing
by-and-by.

Alone now
and waiting.

Gone

the guy who
introduced you to
Erik Satie

Gone
the guy who
gave you a cd
of the most upbeat
Townes Van Zandt

Gone
the guy who
sang to you at the end
of your first date
Georges Brassens

Listen for the
moment your heart stops
missing his voice.
It was worth knowing him
just to hear the song.

In Appreciation of Men

I consider you in battle
against me (our lost unity).
Most times, I calculate my own
defeat. Even the smallest of your kind
is scrappy beyond my comprehension.

We women resign ourselves to
coy pursuit and showy displays
We pretend to ignore
your carved jaw, strong shoulders,
your expert hands. We hide
in a forest of multitasking.

We ignore your heavy voice.
We have so much to do, and so
we measure mystery, veering
toward pretend. At your best you are
yourself. You remind us that we
are good just as we are.

You have the advantage opening
jars, which you do just because we ask.
Thanks for all of the couches you've moved,
the times you've walked us to our cars
in the dark without asking for anything.

It's sweet that you depend on us.
and let these differences twine us together
in the moments we are comforted
by your strong arms and wolf eyes.

After Your Parents Break Up

What seam can't be mended
and sewn before this rip ruins?
A gentle stick with a needle, a piercing
followed by a thread of keeping, of joining.
The trail can be visible or hidden,
black thread on yellow or a perfect match.

You can wear it on your birthday.
When you leave home, your mother will
dry her tears with its sleeve. Your dad
can borrow it for your wedding.
When you are alone and groping
for truth, it will keep you warm.

Ask your parents to try.

They keep tearing at this love
dumping tubs of old, molding
leftovers onto the kitchen floor
screaming for the other to clean it up.
But you'll spend your life mopping their mess
with the shreds of their love for you
what they never risked mending.

You are not something left to rot.
These rags are not you. You can
dry your tears on a new hem.
The bath is full of warmth and hope.
Scrub until you smell like flowers.

Love can make you clean.

Any Fine Day

Something like *safe love* should exist,
but it always steps out of the boat
into the storm at sea. Every day
it walks on water, balances belief.
Earthen love stands atop the welling waves.

Any fine day your beloved might betray
you, and you'll see, surprised, by the swirling
eddies you've been stepping over. Any
fine day you might betray your beloved
right back. Love can stand upon the tide

that tries to pull us under, ride the wave
toward a shore where we won't betray, a place
where betrayal won't pull us under
only make us sad and brave enough to say
Forgive us. We do not know what we're doing.

Falling

You are water
falling over
a cliff

her hand is
gravity
pulling
you
to
slick rocks
beneath
you

eroding what she
reckoned
would never change

Erosion

All things stretch to hold her
she melts atop a mountain
she trickles down his slope

a bank guides her gushes
the ground gives way to stream
a rock heart expanding

to make room for her motion
in a gully, in a chasm
filled by torrents of water

a rush of melting snow
cascading against the stone
eroding with joy to admit her.

Part Four

Solos

What Is

The memory of who I was
reminds me
of who I am not

Sifting through dusty hopes
Were these not true?
nonsense ideas
never pursued
what I am is
what is

No matter
how many
wishes were
abandoned
denied

It wasn't me.
No matter how fiery
my forested heart burns
to be her, the *it* girl
who has everything
I ever wanted

Are these fitful
half-hoped dreams
worth the scab?
What will would I
direct my way?
Uriah or David?
Vashti or Esther?
Rachel or Leah?

Val's Birthday Party

The most interesting person
in the room did not speak to you
or to anyone, confusing
the extroverts, those who ease
out anecdotes, never pulled down forked
paths by others' fine tales.

The ping ponging inside her head
distracted her from vibrant words
from the little conversations
happening, surrounding her thoughts
in volley waiting for a lull
long enough for her to conceive
a fine witticism that might
have charmed the whole room of revelers
but the ball pinged across her brain
hitting a wall

the most interesting person
in the room waits for someone
to hear the bouncing sound
of the ball, someone to arrive
ready with paddle, someone to
play a mental game
of ping pong until she can give
herself a voice.

The Louder the Better

--inspired by Dwight Yoakam

Driving on a warm February day
across Kansas I remember why I cry
and consider never taking this road again

the memories drive me crazy, lonely
somewhere we started to sing along
so many hours in the car finding melody

so this is me trying to turn it on, turning
this memory until I'm set loose
onto the blank horizon with spinning

wind turbines etching circles in my mind
about why I turned up alone again
on this highway a thousand miles from time

I don't sing along anymore, all grown up
the words mean nothing and every song
is about me falling again, standing up

Hey Mister! The sun sets at the end of the road
I'll put in a new cd without lyrics
stop at a gas station before I hit empty.

The Blessing of the Cottonwood

The seeds of a cottonwood
float against a cloudless sky

white on blue gliding in the wind
the image lost in the sun's light

on the other side of the orb
it flies brightened and visible

adrift in the air, looking down
on a woman floating on the water

her inflatable raft, hot pink
adrift on the greenish-brown lake

her skin slick with sunscreen
observing the cottony seeds

she wonders how many years
she might lie bikinied on lakes

floating under the sun
among the fluffy seeds

falling, one lands on bare stomach
a soft white-on-tan blessing

a prayer she will be seen again
on a hot summer's day

the sky blue, the breeze soft
and her body just right.

Hating the Sun

I can't remember hating the sun like I do today,
beating us down with its summer scourge.
Hating us. Hurting us. Killing what we
wanted so much to keep alive. Pouring
drought into our hearts.

I saw a tiny cloud cover the sun yesterday.
A little girl said it looked like a continent.
The thirty seconds that it spent hiding
the sun held our attention and made it
massive, like the distance to childhood.

My friends, you all have been clouds for me.
Sadly, many of you have passed
a little too far east, failing to shade me.
Others have been consistent tiny reprieves.
Thank you, even if you were only the hope
of a shadow.

And to that giant thunderhead out west,
always churning then passing me by, I forgive you.

The sun killed the fifty-year-old cedar in my yard.
Can a more generous cloud build tomorrow?

Drink a Glass of Water

When you are tempted to despair
dismissing hope
drawn into gloom

drink a glass of water.
Stare at the puffy clouds
passing over your town.

Walk barefoot in the dewy grass
on a crisp, still morning.
Consider the carved river bed.

Each particle recalls a cloud
snow on distant mountains
canyons carved by catastrophe.

The molecules bear history
livening creation,
destruction and repair.

Like you, the water forgets
hope and triumph
just waiting to be swallowed.

Acedia

Following my own cobweb highways
I spin around puzzles and plans,
aimlessly roaming, hoping for motive

scouring through thousands of small steps
for the one misstep that brought me here,
far from truth, what I most
hoped I could find.

The web strings across my days
attracting all manner
of six-legged wanderers,
that I consume, assuming
that I will be nourished
by what sticks around.

Autobiography

Nineteen
living in the States,
her fourth country
fresh mind, eager ideas
believing everything
she says.
She's talking to me
twenty years her senior.

I marvel at her youth
and feel ordinary
unacquainted with her
spectrum identities
chemical experiments
fatalistic philosophies
that have
evolved for her
into the death of free will.

Me? I am content to accept
my desire for men
satisfied to drink one beer
unflinching in my belief
in God and free will.

I ask of her,
Where is your home?
She says,
I don't have one.

I reckon some experience
can't be sought
some follow you
like the blue sky
stirring you up
like a whirlwind
spinning across open fields.

My directions home
have never moved:
take the last paved road
in the county
turn right at the yield sign
look east in the morning
west in the evening
straight up at night

the stars refuse
to be counted
but demand
to be named
and I'm called to listen.

December Heart

Eyes strewn with lights,
she'll follow any star
of wonder. When her heart
is exposed, its surface
shimmers like snow
glassed and globed.
And shatters like
icicles sharp and cold.

Save a Seat

Save a seat for the mystic
to sit at the table
and enjoy your cheer.
Pour her some wine and ease
the weight of heavy cares.

Let her see your faces
a reprieve from desolate
visions and reddened eyes
withhold your gasp
as she drapes a vision
shawl-like on the back of her chair.
Watch her shiver without it.

Extend your hand, a balm
for healing the brand burned
onto her heart, your palm
healing the fiery, sublime
conversations that cough
up tears, forcing her to
hide within the rock's cleft.

Let her come to the party
fragile and wild. Ignore
the glass globe she carries
like a purse full of song
and light that all suspect
and none perceive.

Still

I am
sitting still,
now
an act of great will.
The season's change
giving me calm
courage to be
useless in the cool morning air
of October
underneath a hackberry tree.

I am
so still,
the birds' rustle
among the drying leaves startles me.
Each robin furiously harvesting
berries, them that I have never
considered, never watched
their harvest colors

pick   pick
       pick
and
                  hop
hop
      hop

with all of their autumn
kin buzzing, gleaning,
and storing

I am
a lightsome still
creature below.
I neither sow
nor reap, but sip
hot coffee, letting them
and everyone be.

Part Five

The Congregation

A Pilgrim

On a Palm Sunday, as the world
isolated, I walked my dog
to the church's locked doors
like a pilgrim, exiled

barred and uninvited.
I picked out a pandemic palm
a pale celebration,
without the thronging congregation.

Palm in hand, I processed
and sat down at an outdoor bench
pausing before a statue of Mary
who pulled me in.

We sang,
full-voiced
in our
solitude:

Hosanna to the Son
Of David, the King of Israel
Blessed is he who comes in the
Name of the Lord.

We lingered in the empty lot
singing a hymn of ransom and mercy
the promise made
to our fathers.

Laughter After the Rain

Laughter follows the rain, refusing
the moon her silence
snickering at a joke
only a frog gets
something about dying
buried deep in earth
when the rain calls,
Lazarus,
and the frogs come forth.

The Third Decade (of the Rosary)

As my thumb and index finger
crawl their way to the third decade
and pause in the space where a bead
should be for a third mystery,
in its glorious absence
I find the Spirit descending.

He waits for me on Wednesdays

Ascension, a brother bead,
has never strayed, faithfully held
by my fingers, to consider the scarred
hands' reunion with the North Star.
God drawing himself to himself
as creation calls out to Him
for the incarnation, a cynosure of love.

Awaiting the Helper on Wednesdays

The lost bead's story fulfills a vow
I will not leave you orphaned.
Mysteries separated by decades on
a string together ascending and
descending into this space I
add my prayer to be made worthy
of the promises of Christ.

Seeking me on Wednesdays

My prayers end, the beads fold into a purse
dark inside like the night sky filled
with stars resting upon the crucifix.

Nearly There

When I am close—
near the right word
near the true voice
consubstantial
with clear silence

all things sync true
the sea's surface
reflects sunshine
the wind cuts its
face like stained glass

I see the word as a wandering bark
floating and aimless on a still ocean
nearly sailing passed the curve
lost to sight when the true captain
spies it: the star, an ever-fixéd mark.

I can taste tomorrow,
all things made new.

Mud in Your Eye

Coming to the story again, this time
I think, *that was for me. I too can't see.*
The man who was blind then made double-blind
as Jesus covered dim eyes with spit-mud

You are dirty, not because you can't see.
He smeared symbol in his eyes so I'd know
my own need to wash in that pool which when
translated means sent. *Where am I going?*

I ask, *Lord, why am I unclean again?*
My teacher spits in the dirt, and He says,
Here's mud in your eye, which when translated
means, *You're filthy. Come have a drink with me.*

Stories repeating
the truth about me.

The Unsung Song

for me

I am the singer of the unsung song
A song in your heart trying to get out
A song you refuse to live without
I am the singer of the unsung song

I might be an angel descending
or a soft wind that whistles
and spins along lifeless thistles
an eternal song unending

Some days I'm a baby's toes
a sleepy sigh near your head
burial for the long-lived dead
a song without words no one knows

I am the singer of the unsung song
take hold of my hand, we become chorus
if you'll sing with me, they can't ignore us
This song now sung, our tune lifelong.

Canyon

Missing him is
       an empty pain
a hollow space
       reformed
eroded as I live
       the space expands
carving through
       my heart
a canyon
       never empty
while streams
       string through
the bottom
       flowing
filled by souls
       in their flesh
the empty space
       recalling
the departed
       like water
they flow
       into new bodies
leaving me cleft
       but sure
assured and certain
       of a sea
where streams
       collect and fill
the hollows'
       deep divide

Advent: The Gift

After Eucharist
during advent I kneeled
in my pew. The shoot from
the stump of Jesse kicked

inside of me, light seeped
through tiny cracks and what
I held tottered and sloshed
inside my waiting heart.

It grew heavy and fell.
My jar shattered on the tile.
All I knew of comfort
and joy puddled on the floor

it had held as much as
my heart could hold. So full
now too small to hold all.
Near shards of brokenness

I find a pearl, treasure
ever-expanding.
Across the church the priest
closes the door to the

tabernacle, pausing
kneeling before the drip
of love eroding me
carving new cracks each time

the earthen vessel breaks
the gift remakes me.

Lost Guide

There will be times when I am unable
to recall the next line. I will begin
the *Gloria*, and forget all the words.
This will happen when I am the cantor
at a Saturday night mass, my voice lost.

We praise you, we bless you; won't come to mind,
but the people of the parish will sing
my voice, becoming unnecessary,
one of many. When I refuse or can't,
they will, and the sound of their full voices

is a rainbow over the Canyonlands
bending toward an island in the sky.
I'm standing at the edge of the mesa
crying at the horizon's lone raincloud
the edge of the sky dazzled by color.

Their voices call me back to the old song
our offering joined by saints and angels
in the new earth and the new heaven where
the lyrics are known, written in the sky
And the words smell like rain.

Acknowledgements

There are so many expressions of gratitude owed, I feel certain to forget someone or something important. Nevertheless, here goes.

Thank you so much to Christopher Tompkins for inviting me to be a part of his community of poets at Darkly Bright, and the other poets from our virtual community.

Thank you to Joshua Sturgill for his meaningful and thoughtful edits and criticisms during the draft process of this book.

Thank you to Ramona McCallum for being my on-the-spot reader for so many of these poems and for so many years. Also thanks to Jera McGraw, Valarie Smith, Christopher Lobmeyer, and Joan Lobmeyer for sitting through readings while I was working through edits.

Thank you to Matthew Lobmeyer for help with the cover art. Also, thank you to Matthew Lobmeyer and Joanna Reese for reading through a draft and providing some final edits.

There are many more people to thank and acknowledge, but I'll save those for when I see you face to face.

Previously published works
The poems "Hating the Sun" and "What You Want" were previously published at the *Coop* website. "Hating the Sun" appeared in *Kansas Time + Place: An Anthology of Heartland Poetry*.

The poems "Groundhog Day," "Still," "St Sebastian in the Kitchen," "Save a Seat," "Strange Parts," "What the Neighbors See," "The Violent," "Advent: The Gift," "Drizzle in the Flint Hills," "Mud in Your Eye," "Acedia," and "Every Days" were previously published at the *Darkly Bright Press* website.

About the Poet

At the edge of the middle, Linda Lobmeyer was born and raised on a farm in southwest Kansas. She received her B.A. from Kansas State University in English literature with a minor in agronomy and her J.D. from Washburn Law School. She lives in southwest Kansas and works in the legal profession. In addition to writing, she enjoys the outdoors, the water, road trips, singing, and downtime with friends and family.